Hallowed Halls

Seamus Harkin

First published in 2010 by Albertane Publications

ISBN

Copyright © Seamus Harkin 2010

Seamus Harkin has asserted his right under the Copyright, Designs and Patents Act 1988 to be identified as the author of this work.

All rights reserved.
No part of this publication may be reproduced, stored in or introduced into a retrieval system, or transmitted, in any form, or by any means (electronic, mechanical, photocopying, recording or otherwise) without the prior permission of the publisher.

All images contained in this publication have been created by the author.

Hallowed Halls

Seamus Harkin
Albertane Publications Copyright © 2010
Telephone +353 74 913 8033

Acknowledgements

I wish to thank Canon David WT Crooks, MA., BD, for his permission to use information taken from his book, Living Stones, published in 2001.

I am also grateful for information taken from the Raphoe Roman Catholic Church directory.

Thanks to Rev Jim Lamont for his help on the Presbyterian Churches and many other people who helped me in all sorts of other ways.

Thanks also to Shaun Mc Bride of Buszone Media for the design and lay-out of the book and to Janet Harkin for editing and for her much appreciated advice.

And last, but by no means least, thanks to my wife Tessie who travelled around the county with me to keep me and all my notes in order.

St. Columba, Cashel

This is the Church of Ireland Church dedicated to St. Columba in Cashel, Creeslough. Built in 1847 this little Church nestles nicely amongst the fields and whins in the valley that runs down from Duntally wood towards the sea near Doe Castle.

St. Michael the Archangel, Creeslough

Here we have the Roman Catholic Church of St. Michael the Archangel, Creeslough, which was built in 1972. This modern style church was designed by Liam McCormack and takes its inspiration from Muckish Mountain, in whose shadow it sits.

Franciscan Friary & Chapel, Ards

Ards House was built in 1708, by the Wray's whose family came from Yorkshire, England. In 1780 they sold the House and Land to the Stewart's, later known as the Stewart Bams. In 1930 the old mansion, Ards House was taken over by the Capuchin Franciscan Order, 1931 this became the Novitiate and Theological Seminary.

St. John's, Ballymore

The Church of Ireland St. John's Ballymore was built 1752. It is a beautiful church and is situated on high ground with a breathtaking view of Muckish.

Presbyterian Church, Dunfanaghy

At the entrance to Dunfanaghy village stands the most spectacular piece of architecture you will see any where around - Dunfanaghy Presbyterian Church. It was built in 1868, the church enhances the approach to the picturesque sea-side village of Dunfanaghy.

Holy Cross, Dunfanaghy

This is Holy Cross Roman Catholic Church, best viewed from the top of the town with Muckish Mountain in the back ground. Holy Cross was built in 1898. It is said that the devil would find it difficult to enter Dunfanaghy as there is a church on all the approach roads.

Holy Trinity, Dunfanaghy

At the other side of Dunfanaghy, on the Horn Head road, is the Church of Ireland, Holy Trinity Church. This is a beautiful stone built church built in 1873.

St. Paul's, Raymunterdoney

Here is Raymunterdoney Church of Ireland, St. Paul's, built in 1805

St. Finian's, Falcarragh

This is St. Finian's Roman Catholic Church in Falcarragh. This is a spacious, modern style church built in 1982, which can accommodate a large congregation.

St. Anne's, Tullaghobegley

Here on the hill-side is Tullaghobegley Church of Ireland Church of St. Anne. It's the only church that I know of which has an old metal stove in the middle of the aisle. It was built in 1820.

Christ The King, Gortahork

In the village of Gortahork is the Roman Catholic church of Christ The King. This very roomy church was built on a raised platform and really enhances the village of Gortahork. As this church is in the Gaeltacht the Irish name is Chríost Rí. It was built in 1953.

Mhuire Na nGras, Innishbofin

On the road from Gortahork to Bloody Foreland on the coast road at Meenlaragh you will see the Island of Inis Bó Finne (Innishbofin). On this island is a Roman Cathlotic Church of Mhuire Na nGras (Mother of Grace). It was built in 1965.

........on guard

Colmcille Naofa, Tory Island

North from Innishbofin lies Tory Island. Here you see the little Chapel of Cholmcille Naofa (St. Colmcille). It was built in 1857.

Colmcille Naofa, Cnoc Fola

This is the Roman Catholic Church of Cholmcille Naofa (St. Colmcille) at Cnoc Fola. This church has a lovely setting on top of the hill looking down on Gweedore. It was built in 1933.

Teach Pobail Mhuire, Derrybeg

Here is the Roman Catholic Church in Derrybeg: Teach Pobail Mhuire (Mary's Chapel) built in 1972. Derrybeg is on the west side of Bloody Foreland, down in the valley.

Church of St. Patrick, Bunbeg

In Bunbeg is the Church of Ireland Church of St. Patrick built in 1844.

Chroí Ró - Naofa, Dunlewey

Here we see the beautiful stone church in Dunlewey, standing out against the back drop of Mount Errigal Mountain and the Poisoned Glen, making it one of the most picturesque churches in the Diocese. This is the Roman Catholic Church Chroí Ró - Naofa (Church of the Secret Heart) which was built in 1873.

Pádraig Naofa, Crolly

Here on the hill-side is the Roman Catholic Church Phádraig Naofa; Min Uí Bhaoill (St. Patrick), built in 1938. It is situated above Crolly in a very rugged setting with spectacular scenery.

.......midday rest

St. Mary Star of the Sea, Annagry

We are now in the village of Annagry, on the road from Crolly to Burtonport. This is the Roman Catholic Church; St. Mary Star of the Sea built in 1895.

St. Andrew's Chapel of Ease, Carrickfinn

This is Carrickfinn and we see the Church of Ireland church in the parish of Gweedore. This little chapel is St. Andrew's Chapel of Ease which is set in magnificent scenery at Carricfinn where you can often find sheep grazing around its walls. It was built in 1857.

St. Mary's, Kincasslagh

On the road to Burtonport we come to the Roman Catholic Church of St. Mary's at Kincasslagh. It sits on the sea-side in view of Cruit Island and was built in 1854.

St. Columba's, Burtonport

We have now arrived in Burtonport at St. Columba's Roman Catholic Church. Built in 1898 the church isn't far from the ferry which takes you to Aranmore Island.

St. Crone's, Aranmore

Here we are on Aranmore. This is the Roman Catholic Church of St. Crone's which was built 1825. It sits on the edge of the sea in a most beautiful Island setting.

St. Crone's, Dungloe

On the outskirts of Dungloe town is the Roman Catholic Church of St. Crone's. This is a modern church built in 1980 and is very spacious with good car parking facilities.

St. Crone's, Dungloe

Below the town of Dungloe along the sea front, stands this beautiful little church. This is St. Crone's Church of Ireland, built in 1844.

St. Conal's, Doochary

This is Doochary and we see the Roman Catholic church of St. Conal's, built in 1896.

St. Patrick's, Meenacross

We are still in the parish of Dungloe. This is the Roman Catholic Church of St. Patrick at Meenacross, built in 1932.

St. Bridget's, Lettermacaward

We now arrive in Lettermacaward and this is the Roman Catholic Church of St. Bridget's.

Church of Ireland, Lettermacaward

This is the Church of Ireland church in Lettermacaward which was built about 1788-1791.

St. Conal's, Portnoo

Here we are in the village of Portnoo. This is a most beautiful seaside area and right out on the headland stands St. Conall's Church of Ireland, built in 1828.

........the hope of summer

St. Conal's, Kilclooney

We now move back towards Ardara where we come to Kilclooney and here we find the Roman Catholic Church of St Conal's.

Church of Ireland, Glenties

This is the village of Glenties. In the middle of the town we turn right where we see the Church of Ireland Parish church of Glenties, built in 1860.

St. Connell, Glenties

On the Ardara end of the town we find the Roman Catholic Church St. Connell. This is a modern church with a very unusual roof; you could say that the roof is the church. It was built in 1974.

The Holy Family, Ardara

In Ardara there are three churches - this is the Roman Catholic Church of The Holy Family in Ardara.

St. Conall, Ardara

This is the Church of Ireland Church of St. Conall. Built in 1833 and was restored in 1908.

Methodist Church, Ardara

Here at the top of the town on a lovely raised site is the Methodist church, built in 1832.

St. Patrick's, Meenanery

Taking the steep breathtaking road up Glengesh Pass we arrive at Meenaneary. Here we find a small Roman Catholic Church, St. Patrick's built in 1964.

Naomh Columba, Glencolmcille

Once over the pass we descend to the beautiful village of Glencolmcille. In the centre of the village is the Roman Catholic Church of Naomh Columba (St. Columba), built in 1854.

St. Columba, Glencolmcille

Down in the valley below the village in a most picturesque setting is the Church of Ireland church of St. Columba. This church was built in 1828.

St. Columba, Carrick

Taking the Killybegs road out of Glencolmcille we come to the village of Carrick. Here is the Roman Catholic Church St. Columba, built in 1858.

Carta Naofa, Kilcar

Following on the road from Carrick to Killybegs we come to the Roman Catholic church in Kilcar. This is Charta Naofa, built in 1904.

St. Mary of the Visitation, Killybegs

Here in the town of Killybegs this is the Roman Catholic Church of St. Mary of the Visitation, built in 1884.

St. John's, Killybegs

Still in Killybegs we have the Church of Ireland church of St. John. This church is situated high in the town and was built in 1828.

St. Joseph & St Conal, Bruckless

This is the Roman Catholic Church of St. Joseph and St. Conal at Bruckless, it was built in 1911.

St. Peter's, Bruckless

Here is the Church of Ireland Church of St. Peter, this old church fits in well in this rural countryside. It was built in 1826.

Methodist, Dunkineely

In the village of Dunkineely is the Methodist church, built in 1854.

St. Naul's, Ardaghey

This is the Ardaghey Roman Catholic Church of St. Naul, built in 1895.

St. John the Evangelist, Inver

Here we see the beautiful setting of the Inver Church of Ireland church, St. John the Evangelist, built in 1807.

Methodist Church, Inver

Outside the village of Inver is the very peaceful setting of the Methodist Church, built in 1881.

St. Mary's, Frosses

In the village of Frosses this is the Roman Catholic church of St. Mary, built in 1892.

The Holy Redeemer, Drimarone

This is the Roman Catholic church, The Holy Redeemer, at Drimarone. This church was built in 1840.

Sacred Heart, Mountcharles

Just below the village of Mountcharles is the Roman Catholic church of the Sacred Heart built in 1879.

Church of Ireland, Mountcharles

Not far from the village is the Mountcharles Church of Ireland, built in 1860.

St. Mary's, Killymard

This is the Killymard Roman Catholic Church of St. Mary's, built in 1984.

Church of Ireland, Killymard

Here we see the Church of Ireland church of Killymard, built in 1826 and rebuilt in 1891.

Christ Church, Lough Eske

On the shores of Lough Eske sits the Church of Ireland church, Christ Church. This is a lovely old church situated overlooking the lake with views of the Bluestack Mountains.

Presbyterian Church, Donegal Town

On the outskirts of Donegal Town is the Presbyterian church, built in 1886.

Methodist Church, Donegal Town

Not far from that we find the Methodist Church.

Church of Ireland, Donegal Town

In Donegal town is the Church of Ireland church, built in 1828.

Four Masters, Donegal Town

On the Ballybofey road out of Donegal Town we come to this magnificent piece of architecture, the Four Masters Church. This is the Roman Catholic Church of St. Patrick, built in 1931.

Church of Ireland, Laghey

Near the village of Laghey we come to the Church of Ireland church, built 1843.

Presbyterian Church, Laghey

This is the Rathneeny 1st Donegal Presbyterian Church near Laghey, it was built in 1801.

Chapel of Ease, Laghey

This is the Laghey Barr Roman Catholic Chapel of Ease situated on the hillside above Laghey.

Bridgetown Gospel Hall, Laghey

On the main road from Laghey to Ballintra, turing off to the left, we find the Bridgetown Gospel Hall.

Methodist Church, Ballintra

Here in the village of Ballintra this is the Ballintra Methodist church.

Church of Ireland, Drumholm

Up the road a little is the Church of Ireland church in the Drumholm Parish. It was built in 1795 and remodelled in 1854.

St. Bridgid's, Ballintra

This is the Ballintra Roman Catholic Church of St. Bridgid, built in 1845.

Immaculate Heart of Mary, Rossnowlagh

Off to the right on the road between Ballintra and Ballyshannon is the Franciscan Community Chapel of the Immaculate Heart of Mary, built in 1952.

Presbyterian Church, Rossnowlagh

Not far from the Franciscan Chapel is the Rossnowlagh Presbyterian Church.

St. John's, Rossnowlagh

This is the Rossnowlagh Church of Ireland church. St. John's was built in 1831

St. Anne's, Ballyshannon

On the highest site in Ballyshannon and visible on entering the town from the Ballintra side, stands St. Anne's Church of Ireland church. It was built in 1795 and was rebuilt in 1841

St. Patrick's, Ballyshannon

Here is the Roman Catholic Church of St. Patrick, built in 1848, overlooks the town of Ballyshannon.

St. Mary's, Cashelard

This is the Roman Catholic Church of St. Mary's at Cashelard, built in 1898.

St. Agatha, Clar, Donegal Town

On the road towards Ballybofey we come to the Clar Roman Catholic Church of St. Agatha, built in 1871.

Church of the Ascension, Meenglass

Nestled in a forest on the hillside we see this quaint little Church of Ireland Church of the Ascension at Meenglass, built in 1962.

St. John's, Kilteevogue

This is the Kilteevogue Church of Ireland Church of St. John, built about 1879.

Our Lady of Perpetual Succour, Cloughan

Here we have the Roman Catholic Church of Our Lady of Perpetual Succour at Cloughan, built in 1828.

St. Joseph, Letterbrick

This is the Roman Catholic church of St. Joseph, Letterbrick, built in 1971.

Cholmcille Naofa, Fintown

Continuing onto the village of Fintown we see the Roman Catholic Church of Cholmcille Naofa (St. Colmcille) built in 1988.

The Holy Family, Edeninfagh

Not far from the Reelin Bridge is the Roman Catholic Church of The Holy Family in Edeninfagh. This church was built in 1906.

Church of Mary Immaculate, Stranorlar

We make our way through Ballybofey and as we come to the bridge we see the Roman Catholic Church in Stranorlar. This is the Church of Mary Immaculate, built in 1867.

Reformed Presbyterian Church, Stranorlar

In the middle of the town of Stranorlar we see the Reformed Presbyterian church, built in 1877.

Church of Ireland, Stranorlar

Staying on the Lifford road we come to the Chruch of Ireland Church which was built around 1733 and was upgraded a few times since then.

Presbyterian Church, Stranorlar

On the Letterkenny road at the end of the town we see the Stranorlar Presbyterian Church built in 1906.

St. Patrick's, Drumkeen

About half way between Stranorlar and Letterkenny we come to Drumkeen. Here we find the Roman Catholic church of St. Patrick, built in 1843.

Presbyterian Church, Donaghmore

This is the Donaghmore Presbyterian Church built in 1977

St. Patrick's, Donaghmore

On the outskirts of Convoy we see the Church of Ireland Church of St. Patrick. This church was built sometime in early 1700 with major renovations carried out in 1864.

Presbyterian Church, Carnone

Not far from the village of Convoy we find the Carnone Presbyterian church, built in 1868.

Reformed Presbyterian, Convoy

At a secluded corner beside the river we see the Convoy Reformed Presbyterian Church.

St. Ninian's, Convoy

In the village of Convoy is the Church of Ireland Church of St. Ninian. This church is situated on the village green and was built 1824.

Presbyterian, Convoy

On the high road above the village of Convoy we find the Convoy Presbyterian church, built in 1903.

St. Mary's, Convoy

On the outskirts of Convoy is the Roman Catholic Church of St. Mary's, built in 1973

Magheracorran Gospel Hall, Convoy

Situated in the midst of farm land not far from the village of Convoy is the Magheracorran Gospel Hall.

St. Eunan's, Raphoe

Entering the town of Raphoe we see on the right the Roman Catholic Church of St. Eunan, built in 1878.

Presbyterian Church, Raphoe

Next we see the very impressive building which is the Raphoe Presbyterian Church, built 1876.

………a winter tide

St. Eunan's Catherdral, Raphoe

Going on through the town past the Diamond we see the Church of Ireland Cathedral Church of St. Eunan's, Raphoe. This historical church dates back to the 17th century and many renovations were carried out on the building since then, with major work being done in 1893.

Congregational Church, Raphoe

We continue through Raphoe where we come to the Raphoe Congregational church.

Presbyterian Church, Ballylennon

This is Ballylennon Presbyterian Church.

St. Columba's, Craigadooish

This is Craigadooish St. Columba's Church of Ireland Chapel of Ease which dates from 1898.

St. Bathin's, St. Johnston

Here we see the Roman Catholic Church of St. Bathin's at St. Johnston, built in 1857.

Presbyterian Church, St. Johnston

This is the St. Johnston Presbyterian church, built in 1849.

Church of Ireland, Carrigans

At the end of the village of Carrigans is the Church of Ireland church, built in 1765.

The Immaculate Conception, Killea

This is the Roman catholic Church of The Immaculate Conception at Killea. This church was built in 1954

Presbyterian Church, Crossroads

This is the Crossroads Presbyterian Church.

Presbyterian Church, Monreagh

This is Monreagh Presbyterian Church. The parish was founded in 1644.

St. Baithin's, Taughboyne

This is Taughboyne St. Baithin's Church of Ireland which dates from 1627.

Church of All Saints, Newtowncunningham

At the entrance of Newtowncunningham we see the Church of Ireland Parish Church of All Saints, built in 1722. This is the only church in the Raphoe Diocese with a Lych Gate. The Lych Gate was used by coffin bearers to place the coffin inside while waiting for the priest and the rest of the funeral cortege.

Church of All Saints, Newtowncunnigham

This is the Newtowncunningham Roman Catholic Church of All Saints. This church was built in 1999 and resembles the shape of a boat.

Presbyterian Church, Newtowncunningham

Further on at the junction road leading into the village we see the Newtowncunningham Presbyterian church, built in 1881.

Church of Ireland, Manorcunningham

This is the Manorcunningham Church of Ireland Parish Church of Raymonchy which was built in 1792.

1st Ray Presbyterian, Manorcunningham

Further on outside the village is the First Ray Presbyterian church, built in 1746.

2nd Ray Presbyterian, Manorcunningham

Continuing on we see the Second Ray Presbyterian church, built in 1849.

St. Columba's, Drumoghill

This is the Roman Catholic Church of St. Columba at Drumoghill which was built in 1835.

Church of the Irish Martyrs, Letterkenny

This is the Roman Catholic Church of The Irish Martyrs at Gortlee. This is a modern church built in 1994.

Presbyterian Church, Letterkenny

Here in the Main St. Letterkenny is the Letterkenny Presbyterian Church which was built in 1640.

Gospel Hall, Church Lane, Letterkenny

Turning up Church Lane we see here on the left the Letterkenny Gospel Hall, built in 1895.

St. Eunan & St. Columba Cathedral, Letterkenny

Overlooking the town is the Roman Catholic Cathedral of St. Eunan and St. Columba. This Cathedral was built in 1901.

Church of Ireland, Letterkenny

Across the car park from the Cathedral we see the Church of Ireland church. This church dates back to 1636 having been upgraded many times since with the last improvement in 1902. These two churches form the centre piece of the town.

St. Columba, Glenswilly

This is the Roman Catholic Church of St. Columba Glenswilly, built in 1840-1.

St. Columba, Churchill

In the village of Churchill is the Church of Ireland Church of St. Columba built in 1819. This church is in a very picturesque setting with views across the valley as far as Inishowen.

St. Colmcille, Glendowan

This is the Roman Catholic Church of St. Colmcille, Glendowan. It was built in 1851.

Presbyterian, Treantagh

Not far from Kilmacrennan is the Treantagh Presbyterian church, built in 1902.

St. Columba's, Kilmacrennan

This is the Kilmacrennan Roman Catholic Church of St. Columba, built in 1903.

St. Finian & Mark, Kilmacrennan

Just over the bridge in Kilmacrennan is the Church of Ireland's St. Finian and St. Mark built in 1846.

St. Columba's, Termon

This is Termon Roman Catholic Church of St. Columba built in 1854.

Presbyterian Church, Leiter

Close to the village of Kilmacrennan is the Leiter Presbyterian Church, built in 1846.

Presbyterian Church, Milford

At the entrance to the town we see the Milford Presbyterian church, built in 1896.

Reformed Presbyterian Church, Milford

Beside this church is the Reformed Presbyterian church, built in 1837 and renovated in 1926.

St. Peter's, Milford

This is the Milford Roman Catholic Church of St. Peter, built in 1960.

St. Mary's, Ramelton

Here we have the Ramelton Roman Catholic Church of St. Mary, built in 1890.

St. Paul's, Ramelton

This is the Ramelton Church of Ireland Church of St. Paul built in 1825.

First Presbyterian, Ramelton

The next church we see is the Ramelton First Presbyterian church, built in 1601.

St. Colmcille, Glenallagh

This is the Glenallagh Church of Ireland church of St. Colmcille, built in 1850.

Presbyterian, Rathmullan

In the village we see the Rathmullan Presbyterian Church, built in 1872.

St. Joseph's, Rathmullan

Further on at the edge of the town is the Roman Catholic Church of St. Joseph, built in 1892.

St. Columba's, Killygarvan

This is the Killygarvan Church of Ireland Church of St Columba, built in 1887.

St. Catherine's, Oughterlin

Here is the Roman Catholic Church of St Catherine at Oughterlin, built in 1792.

St. Mary's, Glenvar

Here we see the Roman Catholic Church of St. Mary Glenvar, built in 1862.

Our Lady of Lourdes, Carrowkeel

We now continue on to Carrowkeel here we see the Roman Catholic Church of Our Lady of Lourdes, built in 1957.

Presbyterian Church, Carrowkeel

At the end of the village we come to the Carrowkeel Presbyterian Church.

Church of Christ the Redeemer, Rossnakill

Near the village of Rossnakill in the parish of Clondevaddock is the Church of Ireland Church of Christ the Redeemer. This church dates back to the 17th century and it was restored in 1830.

St. Columba, Massmount

Here is the Roman Catholic Church of St. Columba, Massmount, built in 1800. This church is in a very picturesque setting right at the side of the water.

Church of Ireland All Saints, Portsalon

This is the Church of Ireland All Saints Church, Portsalon, built in 1963.

St. Patrick's, Ballinacrick

This is the Roman Catholic Church of St. Patrick Ballinacrick, built in 1932

St. Mary's, Fanavolty

This is the Roman Catholic Church of St. Mary's, Fanavolty built in 1830.

The Immaculate Conception, Ballyheerin

Here is the Roman Catholic church of The Immaculate Conception, Ballyheerin, built in 1955.

Chapel of Ease, Leatbeg

We come to this quaint little church of Leatbeg. This is a Church of Ireland Chapel of Ease built in 1843 and is the last church in the Fanad peninsula.

The Immaculate Conception, Coole

Here is the Roman Catholic Church of The Immaculate Conception at Coole. This church was built in 1953.

St. Brigid's, Golan

Up on the hillside we see the Roman Catholic Church of St. Brigid's, Golan, built in 1870.

Presbyterian Church, Carrigart

At the entrance to the village we see the Carrigart Presbyterian Church.

Holy Trinity Church, Mevagh

This is the Mevagh Church of Ireland, Holy Trinity Church, Carrigart, built in 1895.

.........reflections at Trá na Rossan

St. John the Baptist, Carrigart

Here we see the lovely stone built Roman Catholic Church of St. John the Baptist, built in 1886.

Stella Maris, Mevagh

This is the Roman Catholic Church of Stella Maris built in 1954. This little church is situated on the hillside over looking Downings and Sheephaven Bay. This church takes us to the end of our tour of the churches in the diocese of Raphoe.